to **Feng Shui**—
it will bring harmony
and happiness to your
home and life.

FENG SHUI

FENG SHUI

DEBRA KELLER

DESIGNED BY DIANE HOBBING

Ariel Books

**Andrews McMeel
Publishing**

Kansas City

Calligraphy copyright © 2003 by Stephanie JT Russell

ISBN: 0-7407-3367-2
Library of Congress Catalog Card Number: 2002111887

FENG SHUI

Imagine a world where everything is connected, where a thread of **energy** flows through all matter tying everything together so the mood of one influences all.

Now look around you. That's the
world in which you live, according
to the principles of **Feng Shui.**

Feng Shui is the ancient Chinese
art of harmonizing your environment to improve your quality of
life, and it has been practiced for
over four thousand years. It's
based on the notion that every-

FENG SHUI

thing teems with **energy** (called **chi**) and all **energy** seeks a state of balance. When active **chi (yang energy)** is in balance with passive **chi (yin energy)**, life is good! Happiness abounds, romance thrives, good health is abundant, and business couldn't be better.

In practicing **Feng Shui**, you can

control the connections around you. By moving a couch or repainting a wall you can rearrange and bend the flow of **chi** to achieve a new harmony and influence your life: find a partner, change careers, become a family, learn how to relax, or simply get a good night's sleep.

FENG SHUI

Feng Shui may not solve every problem, but it's certainly a positive step. Read on to discover some of its secrets, then try them out and see how you feel.

When you're feeling too lethargic to clean the house, clean the house! Accumulated dust slows or even stops the flow of **chi.** A good dusting will renew your **energy,** invigorate your spirit, and stimulate your optimism.

FENG SHUI

An argumentative home may not be the fault of the personalities within, but rather, too much fiery **chi energy** in the south. Try watering it down with a houseplant potted in rich, black soil—if you live with teenagers, you might want to try several!

FENG SHUI

Before you consider a job or career change, surround yourself with glass. The **chi** of glass objects— dishes, vases, marbles—is packed with power, security, and peace. Black glass is best, especially if it holds running water. A black glass aquarium is one of the most influential of all objects, although you may not be able to see any fish.

FENG SHUI

If you're depressed, tired, or out of sorts, eat some pretzels. Salty foods have the most **yang,** and can lift your listless **yin energy** to the rafters.

Next time you're in the mood for passionate romance, cuddle up with your sweetheart on a couch (or big chair) on the east side of a room facing west. It will not only bring the two of you closer, but will also saturate your **chi** with sexual **energy.**

Remember to close the bathroom door. Too much dampness, especially near a bedroom, can drain you of **chi** and leave you feeling bored.

FENG SHUI

The best place for a stove is on the east wall of your kitchen. It might not make you a better cook, but it will likely increase the patience you need to try new recipes.

When it comes to swimming pools, think kidney shaped. Besides being retro chic, they're ideal for stimulating healthy **chi**, especially if they're east of your home.

FENG SHUI

If you have a choice of where to sit during a business luncheon, select a seat that's farthest from the door. It's best if you can sit in a booth, and even better if the booth is against a wall. The inside seat of the last booth on the left is the most **powerful** seat of all.

A theater box seat might be the envy of wealthy Westerners, but, according to **Feng Shui,** it's the worst seat in the house. It's far better to sit facing the stage, especially in the middle of the third row from the back. The flow of **chi** there is ideal—just remember to bring your opera glasses.

FENG SHUI

To make dinner for two more romantic, sit at a small round table. Round tables have the most **yang** and promote a dynamic flow of **chi.** Sharing an unhurried meal at a small round table can lead to untold excitement.

Family dinners are best served around an oval table. The flow of **chi** around an oval table is relaxed and harmonious. Large oval tables have the added benefit of allowing plenty of space between siblings.

FENG SHUI

If you live in a home with a slightly pitched or flat roof, you're living under the element of soil. Soil **energy** is secure and comforting, but too much can lead to lethargy. Keep your soil **energy** balanced with an occasional fire. If you don't have a fireplace, a few candles will do. If you run out of candles, decorate with purple.

25

Shadows absorb **chi** like a sponge. Before you buy or rent a new home, visit it at various times of the day. If it falls under the shadow of a neighboring structure, you might want to reconsider your move. At the very least, hang wind chimes on its dark side to stimulate **chi.**

FENG SHUI

A shiny brass doorknob not only looks good, but it also helps deflect negative **energy.**

North energy is the most calming. If you typically come home from work exhausted and stressed, retreat to your northernmost room. Add a couch, chair, or even a bed to make that room your haven—a rejuvenating place to rest, relax, read a book . . . or perhaps the want ads.

When looking at a stairway through a **Feng Shui** master's eyes, it's easy to see its resemblance to a waterfall. The longer and steeper the stairs, the faster the flow of **chi.** To slow the flow and recirculate **energy,** hang a mirror at the bottom to reflect **chi** upward. If your stairway is near your front door, the mirror can also be used in

FENG SHUI

the Western manner—to check how
you look before you step outside.

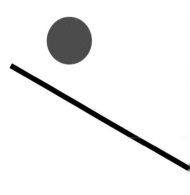

If you're having a hard time focusing at work, try moving closer to your workplace door. But not too close! A desk or workstation too close to a door can attract too much **chi** and make you feel anxious. The best place to work is somewhere in the middle. Just where, though, is something only trial and error can tell.

FENG SHUI

In addition to sometimes numbing your mind, watching TV can also numb your spirit. It's best to sit as far away as you can, and even better if you can face southeast. Best of all, put a houseplant next to your television set. It may not improve the quality of the shows, but it will help improve the room's **energy.**

FENG SHUI

You're going out to dinner with two friends and one has offered to drive. Instead of hoping to snag the front passenger seat, grab the seat behind the driver. That is the seat of security and understanding—the most fortuitous seat in a car.

Although you may enjoy lying in bed and looking at the stars, a bed under a window is not wise according to the principles of **Feng Shui.** Because **chi** flows freely in and out of windows, sleeping under one—especially if you like to sleep with the windows open—can rob you of peace.

FENG SHUI

To strengthen a meaningful relationship, decorate your bedroom with pairs. Two paintings hung side by side over a dresser, two candles on your nightstand, two plants in the same pot—not only will pairs double your romantic **energy**, they'll also reinforce your psychological closeness.

Next time you balance your check-book, balance yourself at the same time. Eat a cookie! Financial accounting is a **yang** activity that can be harmonized with the **yin** of sugar.

FENG SHUI

Plant purple flowers in the south part of your garden to increase your passion and bring social success. For success in business, plant deep red flowers in the west.

Ferns and grasses in the east part
of your garden can help you feel
vital and fresh. Plant creamy
white flowers in the north
to quiet your anxieties
and blanket you in **peace.**

FENG SHUI

Yellow is the color of balance.
Something yellow in the middle of
your home will help keep you
centered. Try a yellow
vase, a yellow pillow,
even a yellow rubber
duck playfully floating
in a bowl of water.

To avoid flushing **chi** down the drain, always keep the toilet lid closed.

FENG SHUI

A bathroom in the south part of your home leaves you vulnerable to being sued. To counteract its negative effects, decorate your bathroom with tall plants and wooden accessories.

The chi of life is constantly changing. To make the most of its continual renewal, change your environment as often as you can. Move furniture, pillows, and rugs at least once a year. Change paint colors whenever you can afford to. Even small changes can make a big difference—a new tablecloth, another basket, or the way you stack

FENG SHUI

your magazines can all invigorate
your spirit.

If you've been wearing out your credit cards, your **chi** might be off kilter. To stop the drain on your income and restore financial harmony, surround yourself with red. Try red flowers, red candles, or your favorite red holiday tablecloth—even if it's the middle of August.

FENG SHUI

The next time you get a cold, baby yourself with chicken soup served in a glass bowl. Because glass is **yang,** it can help balance your **yin** fatigue—and the chicken soup can't hurt either.

The kitchen is the soul of any house, but especially one aided by **Feng Shui.** Ancient Eastern philosophy holds that a healthy diet leads to longevity, and therefore, the kitchen is the center of life. Keep your kitchen clean and uncluttered to encourage a healthy flow of **chi.**

FENG SHUI

Sunlight plays an important role in **Feng Shui.** It lights the dark to keep **chi** from stagnating and it dries damp places to keep **chi** fresh and clean. Wherever sunlight shines into your house, throw open your windows and welcome it!

The next time you throw a dinner party, set the mood when you set your table. The color of your table linens can influence the event:

Red for romance

Orange for harmony

Yellow for warmth

Green for activity

FENG SHUI

Blue for communication

Purple for passion

Black for practicality

White for excitement

Gray for dignity

Beige for relaxation

Pink for playfulness

Brown for security

Hang floral prints and wallpaper with rounded patterns to invite more romance into your life. Vertical stripes can increase ambition, but motivation is encouraged by checks. Stars and pointed patterns can make you more passionate, but if you want to increase your sexual appetite, only irregular patterned wallpaper will do.

If you've been feeling lonely lately, you might be spending too much time facing north. North **energy** promotes calm and independence, but too much can cause isolation. Balance yourself by spending more time in a south-facing room—southern **energy** enhances communication and an active social life.

FENG SHUI

The best location for a family or playroom is the southeast corner of a home. Southeast **energy** promotes harmony, communication, and creativity. If the family room is located elsewhere, decorate it in harmonious blues and greens.

Besides being fun at a party, colored lights can have a tremendous influence on your life by manipulating the **chi** around you. Try green if you want to build your career; try blue to improve your communication skills. Red will bring out your passionate side, and yellow will help you feel centered.

FENG SHUI

Plantation shutters might be in vogue, but they shut out so much light they virtually halt the flow of **chi.** To balance their **yang energy** and invite **chi** into a shuttered room, decorate it with large cushions.

Don't forget your garage! A cluttered garage is a haven for stagnant **chi**. A **Feng Shui** master would arrange his garage with the heaviest items stored in the back, smaller items shelved on the left side, things with wheels on the right, and a large open space in the middle. As for whatever does not fit, he'd have a garage sale!

FENG SHUI

Sharp corners tend to spin **chi** outward in streams of unhealthy **energy.** If you're in the path of one of these shafts, your **chi** can be knocked off balance, leaving you irritable, disoriented, or even ill. Avoid sharp-edged furniture if you can, or soften sharp edges with tablecloths or the draping tendrils of houseplants. If you can't avoid

FENG SHUI

the path of a point, at least
protect yourself with something
reflective, like a silver locket or a
shiny belt buckle.

If you're considering changing jobs, you might want to first change your furniture. East is the direction associated with careers—rearrange your furniture so you sit facing east and you might see a better future.

FENG SHUI

Sleeping under a ceiling fan could be an insomniac's worst nightmare, as it stirs up your **chi.** Turn the fan off at night (if it's hot, skip the covers).

Sea salt tends to absorb **energy** in the same way table salt absorbs moisture. If you live with active children or pets, keep a bowl of sea salt on a high shelf or tucked behind a piece of furniture.

FENG SHUI

Cabinets and cupboards are full of **yin energy,** whereas home offices are primarily **yang.** To balance the driving **energy** of a home office, add plenty of file cabinets. Not only will they help keep you organized, but they'll also keep you from feeling overworked.

Chimes, bells, and gongs have long been used to invigorate **chi,** especially in damp, dark places. Hang wind chimes near pools and garden fountains. Hang strings of bells from bathroom doorknobs. Ring a gong in the center of your home to get **chi** flowing throughout—and perhaps call your family to dinner?

It's a good idea for frustrated students to balance their studies **(yang)** with a little creative play, the more imaginative **(yin)** the better. If that doesn't help achieve better grades, a bowl of ice cream **(yin)** might work.

FENG SHUI

Your connection to earth's **energy** begins under your feet, so consider your floor covering carefully. Carpets, rugs, ceramic tiles, and plant fibers all slow the flow of **chi** and make a home more relaxing. Stone, glass, and metal encourage **chi** and create excitement. Wood is generally considered neutral, whereas plastic tends to stop the

FENG SHUI

flow of **chi** altogether and should
be avoided—or covered with something else.

If you like being the center of attention, sit north facing south at your next party. It's the most socially outgoing seat in a room.

The more separation between your home and street the better, according to **Feng Shui.** A porch, hedge, trellis, fence, or meandering front path will help protect you from negative **chi.** If you don't have that much room to spare, a few spiny cacti under a street-side window (or on a windowsill) will keep both negative **chi** and thieves at bay.

FENG SHUI

Pastel colors and soft upholstered furniture can help you relax and wind down. But too much softness can make you feel listless and weak. If you find yourself feeling overly tired, boost your **chi** by adding something long and green: a green-striped pillow; a tall, leafy plant; or a bushy bouquet in a tall, thin vase—flowers optional.

To help calm active children, position their beds so their heads are to the north. You may not be able to quiet their days, but their nights will be infused with tranquillity.

FENG SHUI

Fluorescent lights might be more cost effective than incandescent bulbs, but they tend to absorb **chi**. To encourage the flow of **chi** while saving on your electric bill, light candles.

A red front door can lift spirits, enhance romance, encourage leadership, and invite wealth. When painted on a front door, no other color can do more.

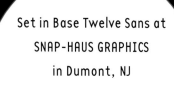

Set in Base Twelve Sans at

SNAP-HAUS GRAPHICS

in Dumont, NJ

Book design by Diane Hobbing